A Thousand Paths to Love

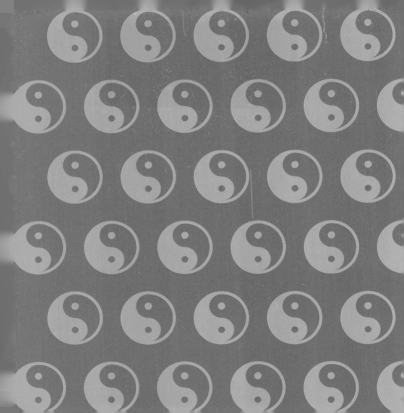

A Thousand Paths to
love

David Baird

spruce

Contents

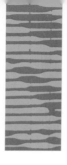

Introduction

What is love?
Books and songs, films, poems, roses, candy, even days have been dedicated to it, but what do we understand of love? What part does love play in our lives, and what is our part in love? Where do we find love and what forms might it take? How do we give love to others, or ourselves for that matter? Who, what, and why do we love?

There are as many answers to the questions about love as there are lovers to ask them. Love has ever delighted and perplexed, inspired and confounded. Here within these pages we shall visit love from every imaginable angle in an attempt to show how this celebrated and mysterious emotion has been, and ever will be, the one enduring obsession of humankind.

What is Love?

Love is a promise
that is never broken.

Love is a fortune you
will never be able to spend.

Love is a seed that
grows anywhere.

Love is a light
that never fades.

Love is the creator of our greatest memories and the foundation for our fondest dreams.

Love is everything you never knew you always wanted.

Love is only known to those who love.

Do not worry about finding love. Love will find you when the time is right.

The greatest
gift we can
possibly give
to another is
a portion of
ourself.

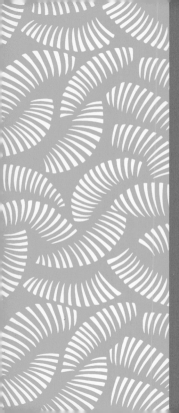

Love is a song that cannot be sung solo.

To love is to admire with the heart; to admire is to love with the mind.

Love is the greatest instinct—follow your heart.

There is no reasoning with the heart.

Love is a dream from which we need never wake.

To fear love is to fear life.

Love is a game with no rules, and the winner takes all.

The only way to learn about love is by loving.

Remember: once you have given love you can never take it back.

Love is a gift
that is worth
nothing unless
given freely.

**A gift wrapped with love
is never too small.**

A life lived in love is one worth living.

You must love with *all* your heart.

Love is the key to the gate of happiness.

Love is a lovely and fearful thing.

Love not only makes the world go round; it is what makes the ride worthwhile.

Love cannot live alone.

Love is like the ocean, it ebbs and flows—the ocean is never full of water, and the heart is never full of love.

What is important is that
one is capable of love.

Love is perhaps the only glimpse
we are permitted of eternity.

It is said that lovers don't just
finally meet somewhere; they
are in each other all along.

Great love takes great daring.

Risk all for love,
if your love is real.

The greatest
happiness of life
is the conviction
that we are
loved—loved
for ourselves or,
rather, loved in
spite of ourselves.

You don't love a person because
they are beautiful; they are beautiful
because you love them.

Never underestimate
the power of love.

Love is the iron fist in the velvet glove.

Love is the sweetest gift of all,
whether we give it or receive it.

**The way to love anything is
to realize that it may be lost.**

Love is as fragile as a sparrow's wing.

The heart has its reasons that reason does not know at all.

When we look back on our lives, we find that those things we did in the spirit of love represent the moments we were truly alive.

Love conquers all.

Music is love in search of a word.

Love is an orchestra.

The greatest glory of humankind is the
love of one human being for another.

When you feel nothing, you are not alive at all.
Be brave—allow yourself to feel love.

A moment of life spent in love is worth
the rest of life spent without it.

Love is worth most when it costs nothing.

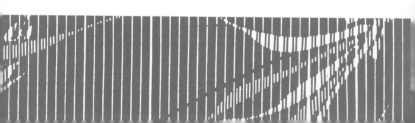

Love is not finding
the perfect person,
but finding the
imperfect person
perfect.

No one is poor who is loved.

No one is ugly who is loved.

No one is foolish who is loved.

Love is the greatest transforming power.

The heart sees what is invisible to the eye.

The greatest pain is caused by the absence of a loved one.

Love gives us
strength to endure.

If you want to give love,
first love yourself.

Holding you,
I hold everything.

We are all capable of loving,
and of being loved.

Love is a taste of eternity.

Love makes the heart strong
when the body is weak.

Once loved, always loved.

Time takes on another meaning
for those of us in love.

Love is the strongest thing
in the world.

**Love has the power to cast
light in the darkness.**

Love pains and pleases
in equal measure.

Love
coats
the eyes
with
desire
and
cloaks
the heart
in grace.

When my love is near, I know it with
every fiber of my body.

We can only forgive to the extent
to which we love.

Those who cannot forgive cannot love.

Love does not bear grudges.

The most beautiful things in the world can only be felt with the heart.

Love is the elixir of youth.

Love itself will provide the strength to bear the loss of love.

Passion is an unquenchable thirst.

Love is wanting what we have, not what we can't have.

Whose is the greater gift: those who give without loving, or those who give their love?

No pleasure in life
can compare with the
pleasurable pains of love.

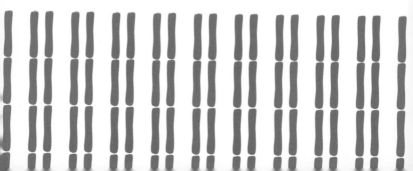

Love given with conditions is no love at all.

Love like you'll never be hurt.

Love grows by giving.

The love we give away
is the only love we keep.

Trust is the best proof of love.

Love is friendship set to music.

Love is the rhythm of life.

Love is, above all, the gift of oneself.

Love is when you think about someone else more times in a day than you think about yourself.

If you want to be loved, you must love.

True-life love stories never have endings.

You know you're in love when you can't sleep because your reality is better than your dreams.

If I know what love is, it is because of my lover.

The first duty of love is to listen.

What is there to fear in love?

The very reason we exist is to love and be loved.

If we allow ourselves to be afraid of love, we will become afraid of life.

Love is as necessary to life as the air we breathe.

Those who give love gather love.

You can't force someone to love you. All you can do is become worthy of love.

We cannot choose who we love, only whose love we choose to accept.

We love our partners not because they are perfect, but because they are perfect for us.

Couples who
love each other
tell each other a
thousand things
without talking.

Chinese proverb

The greatest happiness there is to be had in life is to love and be loved.

Once it has hold of you,
love never lets go.

Love chooses where it strikes.

Once you have learned to love,
you will have learned to live.

Love makes a fairy tale
out of an ordinary life.

Love is not just a word.

Love is not a single action.

Love is the biggest thing there is—and yet it can fit into the confines of the human heart.

The heart is the garden
where love grows wild.

The person who has everything
is the person who is loved by
the person they love.

Love is breathtaking.

The best relationship is one in which your love for each other exceeds your need for each other.

There are not enough words in any language to describe true love.

Love is
patient.

In life, actions speak louder than words.
In love, the eyes do all the talking.

The surest way to receive love is to give love.

Never hold on too tightly to your love, for that is the surest way to lose it.

Love is an impulse and beyond our control.

**Never think that you can
direct the course of love,
for love directs your course.**

In love it is the heart that
rules the head.

**Reason and love
are strangers.**

Love is that which
cannot be defined.

**One of the most terrifying
things in life is the realization
that we are in love!**

Why should it be
that we all want to
fall in love? And why
should it be that we
all need to feel we
are loved?

Love and Marriage

What greater thing is there than for two human souls to feel that they are joined as one.

Some agonize over the kind of wedding they will have, while those truly in love are happy for any wedding that will join them together.

Love always involves a modicum of risk—anything worth having does.

Love is a question of choice.

How can it be love if we haven't made a conscious decision to accept it? Anything else is just chaos.

Marriage must be built upon a foundation of love.

We must ask ourselves whether our sense of love is so absolute that we would be prepared to risk everything for it.

Love only one in your lifetime and you will be happy.

When we say "I love you," those three little words are the biggest investment we will ever make. We say it in the hope that it will yield great returns, and at the very least that those words will be said back to us with interest.

Absolute love is
an absolute risk.

A word spoken in loving
kindness is worth far more
than any gift.

Love that is based entirely upon the erotic leads to jealousy and revenge.

We all have the potential to throw ourself at a person who will ultimately destroy us.

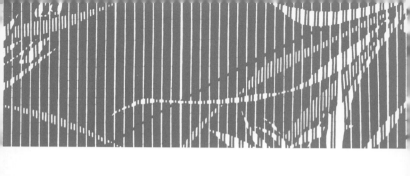

Love is always a question of risk.

Love is always a question of choice.

Love is always a question of faith.

Love is always a question of trust.

We seldom find such sensible people as those who agree with us.

True love can never be built upon self-interest.

Is it possible to love someone that you cannot respect?

The surest way to
be deceived is to
think oneself cleverer
than one's partner.

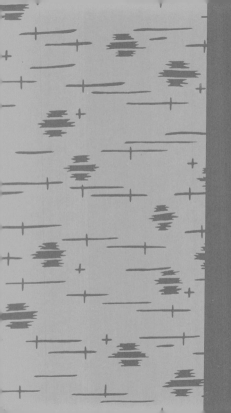

What is
marriage?
A composite
corporate
entity that
faces life
together.

Marriage is a regularizing thing.

Where would opera be without love? Every plot centers upon it.

In opera and theater, love and death share the same dressing room.

Only think about giving, not getting, where love is concerned.

A man is the measure of the things he loves.

Before we fall we must ask
ourselves if our love has a
reason—is it rational?

Love perfects
the imperfect.

Love has no brakes.

The predicament of love—searching for it, falling into it, falling out of it, and living it—is the one abiding obsession of humankind.

The unexamined love is not worth loving.

Those who have found love have found what it is to be alive.

You were born together,
and together you shall be for
evermore…but let there be
spaces in your togetherness.
And let the winds of the
heavens dance between you.

Kahlil Gibran

Marriage has a great many pains.
Celibacy has few pleasures.

Marriage combines the maximum
of temptation with the maximum
of opportunity.

There is no greater robber of wit than
love—if you had wit to begin with.

There is no greater provider of
wit than love—if you had no wit
to begin with.

A lifetime of happiness! No man alive could bear it: it would be hell on earth.

George Bernard Shaw

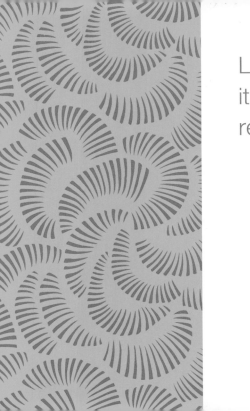

Love is
its own
reward.

Finding pure and complete
sorrow is as impossible as
finding pure and complete joy.

**It is simple to find out how much one
person loves another — ask them. If
they have an answer, then they can't
love much. If they can't answer, then
you know it is serious.**

What an annoying,
mad thing love is!

Lovers speak a language only understood by two.

Those things you love the most about your lover will become the very things that irritate you about them.

Distance is no obstacle to love.

Finding love that is without jealousy is like trying to find a candle that doesn't throw shadows.

The only time on this earth that we are truly, fully alive is that moment when we first fall in love.

If you open your heart, love will open your mind.

Hate is easy—love takes courage.

Absence
sharpens love.
Presence
strengthens it.

We live where we love.

Love inspires love.

The sum of free will plus love is energy.

Wherever love has been,
something remains.

In youth, the union of the flesh works to strengthen the union of souls, which, remaining young and indivisible, strengthens in its turn the union of the flesh in old age and continues after death.

Victor Hugo

All hear what you say.
Friends listen.
Lovers know.

It is not only necessary to love; it is also necessary to say so.

French proverb

Love doesn't become love until we give it away.

Love makes time pass.
Time makes love pass.

Love sustains itself.

Love is the difference between what we need to live and why we need to live.

Love takes commitment, but so does insanity.

People often get divorced over religious differences. Usually one person thinks they are God!

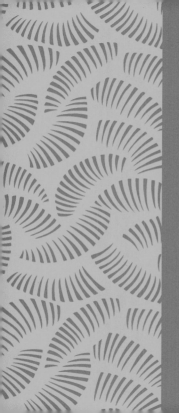

Never strike
your wife—
even with
a flower.
Hindu proverb

Being in love is, of course, a wonderful feeling. Having that love returned is the best experience of all.

A spouse is someone who knows the song in your heart and can sing it back to you when you forget the words.

Mountain is mountain.
Water is water.
Love is love.

When all things become one, that is love.

The reverse
side also has
a reverse side.

A table with
a broken leg
remains a table.

When you are
consumed by
passion, the
meal is yourself.

Always be prepared to see things from your lover's position, even if you don't like the view.

I love, therefore I am worthy of love.

It's easy to fall in love. The hard part is finding someone to catch you.

The bonds of wedlock are so heavy that it takes two to carry them— sometimes three.

What
is left
behind
when two
lovers
cross a
meadow?
Love.

It takes one eye opened to meet your true love, but both eyes closed to keep them.

While the forbidden fruit is said to taste sweeter, it usually spoils faster.

When two people love each other, they don't look at each other—they look in the same direction.

Love is like wet cement—
the longer you stay, the harder
it is to get out. And, when you
finally do get out, you always
leave your shoes behind.

If true love comes knocking only once in a lifetime, make sure to open the doors in your heart when it knocks.

The only thing better than being loved is being told that you are loved.

Love is the secret that people are suspected of until they are married—then they are suspected of no longer being in love.

Marriage is the most pivotal event of one's life, the foundation of happiness or misery.

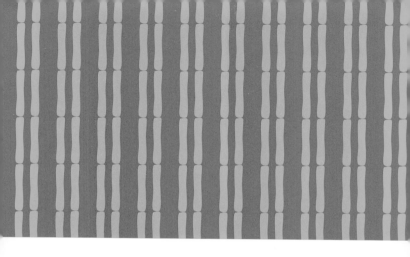

Keep your eyes wide open before marriage, and half-shut afterward.

Marriage is a souvenir of love.

It takes a minute
to have a crush on
someone, an hour to
like someone, a day
to love someone, but
it can take a lifetime
to forget someone.

The best of friends and the greatest of lovers argue. That doesn't mean they don't or can't love.

A woman marries a man expecting he will change, but he doesn't. A man marries a woman expecting that she won't change, and she does.

There are two times that men and women don't understand each other—before marriage and after marriage.

The one who loves least controls the relationship.

If we ever hope to be loved,
we must reveal who we are.

The moment that we need love the most is often the moment that we least deserve it.

A true love is one who overlooks your failures and tolerates your successes.

Love is not competitive.

Those lovers who form the best partnerships bring out the best in each other.

The only true arbitrator of love is time.

Love, friendship, and happiness are inseparable.

Love is to trust someone completely—to like them from the heart.

If we fall in love because someone makes us laugh, what happens when we no longer find them funny?

If we fall in love because someone is beautiful, what happens when that beauty fades?

If we fall in love because someone can provide for us, what happens when they lose their wealth?

Love someone only for their self alone.

Love is having someone who understands your past, believes in your future, and accepts you today just the way you are.

Nothing can diminish the value of love: it provides us with memories that we may treasure for the rest of our lives.

We may never learn all there is to know about love, but every day together will teach us a little more about ourselves.

Love is a meeting of minds, hearts, and spirits.

Love remains love,
despite all its faults.

**In the sweetness of your
love, let there be laughter
and sharing of pleasures.**

Beware of love that seeks to exploit you.

To love and be loved is the greatest and happiest love of all.

Love asks for faith, and
faith asks for firmness.

Love makes all hearts gentle.

To love and be loved is to
feel life from both sides
of the heart.

A man who
fears nothing
loves nothing.

How can love exist if we are not prepared to surrender ourselves to each other? There can be no love without self-sacrifice.

Our feelings just happen. Whether or not we act on these feelings is our choice.

Reduce a person to their chemical value and we are worth very little, but add the love of another person and we become priceless.

A life spent in love is a life well spent.

If you ever expect to be loved, you must reveal who you are.

Love is like war: easy to begin, hard to end.

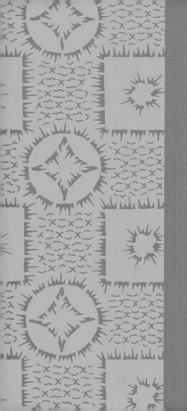

Don't spend your life looking for love. Love will find you.

Love begets love.

It turns out that it's not what we do with our life but who we spend it with that is crucial to our happiness.

The Nature of Love

No matter how good
we try to be, we cannot
be perfect…but our
capacity for love helps
us get a little closer.

The best kind of love is that love
which puts the needs of others
above its own desires.

Love does all for love
and nothing for reward.

There is the kind of love
that makes sacrifices for
the benefit of others.
That is the kind of love that
we should strive for.

If you love somebody, tell them.

Who would believe that something so simple as a kiss could beautify the souls, hearts, and thoughts of mankind?

Shared love is the strongest bond.

Love is its own reward. To expect something from love weakens it.

A simple kiss is capable of wiping out the years and making the heart young again.

Greater love hath no man than this, that a man lay down his life for his friends.

John 15:13

There are no half-measures in love.

When we are in love, one stolen kiss is worth a hundred offered kisses.

A lover fears all that he believes.

People are not where they live but where they love.

True love is the greatest miracle; it has infinite power to transform.

When we are in love, a part of us remains wherever we have been.

Love is real when our heart allows a
part of someone else to grow inside it.

**The greatest story ever lies untold
in the heart of love.**

A smile will always inspire another smile.

Love is blind.

The fate of love is that it always
seems too little or too much.

A thing of beauty
is a joy for ever.

John Keats

When we are in love, we are all
driven by our heart's inspiration.

Love
and tornadoes
can never pass unnoticed.

**Absence makes the
heart grow fonder.**

The love of another is a lovely and fearful thing.

All thoughts, all passions, all delights,
Whatever stirs this mortal frame,
All are but ministers of Love,
And feed his sacred flame.

Samuel Taylor Coleridge

No two love
stories are
the same: the
experience of
love is as unique
as the lover.

In love, if you don't
risk anything, you risk
even more.

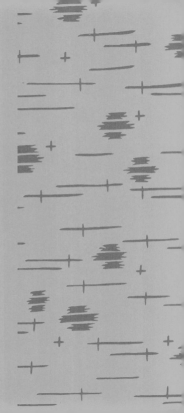

And I would hear yet once before I perish
The voice which was my music—
Speak to me.

Lord Byron

Two people may easily gaze into each
other's eyes, but lovers can look through
each other's eyes and see into each
other's souls.

Once it has known love,
the heart can never again be free.

Love clears and sharpens the vision.

Can the heart ever be filled with love?
Can the ocean ever be filled with water?

**We are more embarrassed to find
ourselves alone after love than we
were to be alone before love.**

Everyone becomes a poet when they
are touched by love.

**Some see beauty in the face, but
true beauty lies within the heart.**

Great care should be taken of love: though it is stronger than steel, it is more fragile than crystal.

While love is heaven on earth, the death of love is living hell.

Whose heart is not provoked by beauty?

My strength matches the depth of your love. My courage matches the depth of my love for you.

My words are more yours than mine.

Come with me, and be my Love,
And we will all the pleasures prove.

Christopher Marlowe

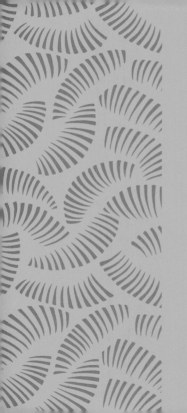

Each moment of a happy lover's hour is worth an age of dull and common life.

A lover's smile is worth a thousand words.

Doubt that the stars are fire;
Doubt that the sun doth move;
Doubt truth to be a liar;
But never doubt I love.

William Shakespeare

A life without love is no more
imaginable than a year without
its seasons.

In love, some are gardeners
and some are florists.

**Love and love alone is the only
reason to love.**

For those who love, time is eternity.

Some people may hear you are talking. A friend will listen to what you have to say. A lover will hang on every word left unspoken.

Everything that deceives also enchants, and vice versa.

The reward for those who love is the knowledge that the love they have given has been lovingly taken.

I love you today less than I will love you tomorrow.

Don't try to explain love—for in doing so you stand to kill it.

Having
the love
of another
person
reminds
us that
we are
special.

The way we feel is the way we wish to be heard.

There are many things in this life that we can do without, but love is not one of them.

Love loud or love in vain.

The most profound relationship any of us will have in this life is the one we have with ourselves.

When I hand you my love,
I hand you my life—my
awakening moments and
all of my dreams.

One doesn't need to be a scholar to
know what love is when it arrives.

Perfect love cannot be described
in words—only actions.

Lovers need each other more than the air they need to breathe.

Unrequited love is the hurt of loving someone and not being loved in return. But the greatest pain of all is loving someone and not being courageous enough to tell them.

Lovers dream of each other to be together even longer than they are when they're awake.

I love you for being you.

I love you for the things you say and do.

I love you for loving me.

I love you for letting me love you.

I love you.

**There is no such thing
as a heart that cannot love.**

The curious thing about
intense love is that it often
resembles hatred more closely
than it does friendship.

Lukewarm love is no love at all.

Time spent together in love is
precious beyond measure.

The promise of love
is warmer than any blanket.

What we love can never
be taken from us.

It is said that if we love someone
we should be prepared to let them go,
for if they come back it proves they
were always ours.

You can't have a rainbow
without rain.

We don't love because we need someone;
we need someone because we love them.

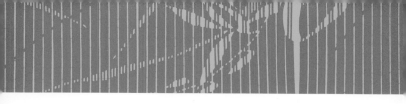

At the beginning of a relationship there are two people. Then they fall in love and become one. But if love dies, and they separate, then all that remains is two torn halves.

The hole that love leaves when it dies is wider and deeper than the hole that was there before love came.

The arithmetic of love is not without its mistakes, for in love two can become one, and two minus one often equals nothing.

Love isn't blind—it is lack of love that is blind.

The language of love is unique,
for a single silent glance can say
a thousand words.

It is love that gives worth
to all things.

None who love are poor.

Love has the power to teach us
things that the most complete and
expensive education could not
teach us in a million years.

Journeys end in lovers meeting.

William Shakespeare

Even unrequited love shows us that we are capable of love, and that is the important thing.

It is said that when two people love each other with all their hearts, if one cries, the other tastes salt.

Enjoy love: without it, life is a sad, pale shadow of itself.

Strength is measured not by holding on, but by letting go.

It is said that we will find it much easier in this life to have ten thousand loves at one time than to have just one.

Love is not measured in time, but depth.

Ask not what love can do for you, but what you can do for love.

Love is never cheap.

Love is friendship set on fire.

Love is neither true nor false—love is love.

Do not enter into love with any great expectations, except the expectation of what you intend to give.

Love is the expression
of simplicity in emotion,
the unattainable
longing that comes
so unexpectedly,
with great subtlety
and bliss.

Luyen Dao

Love is that condition in which
the happiness of another person
is essential to your own.

Love is the language our hearts use
to speak to one another.

Love is the only sane and
satisfactory answer to the
problem of human existence.

To love more is the only way
to heal a broken heart.

Love is the greatest refreshment in life.

Pablo Picasso

You aren't wealthy until you have something money can't buy.

Any love that can be described rationally cannot be heartfelt. There is no accounting for love.

Love can make the wisest of men turn into fools, and fools into the best lovers.

Your first love is the one you miss the most.

Love starts with a smile, grows with a kiss, and ends with a tear.

The love in your heart wasn't put there to stay.
Love isn't love until you give it away.

Love shows us as we are.

In the end, we will remember not the
words of our enemies, but the silence
of those we thought loved us.

Kindness in words creates confidence.
Kindness in thinking creates profoundness.
Kindness in giving creates love.

Teachers open the door, but
you must enter by yourself.

Chinese proverb

Where love can have a happy ending,
jealousy cannot.

Love always hopes.

Love knows no wrong.

Love always trusts.

Love is kind.

Love has faith.

Love perseveres.

Love is humble.

Acts of love can fail as often as they succeed. They are no less the acts of love.

Philosophy
of Love

We are all of us born for love…it is the principal existence and its only end.

Benjamin Disraeli

Love is a butterfly, which when pursued is just beyond your grasp, but if you will sit down quietly it may alight upon you.

Nathaniel Hawthorne

The greatest pleasure of life is love.

William Temple

What greater thing is there for two human souls than to feel that they are joined together to strengthen each other in all labor, to minister to each other in all sorrow, to share with each other in all gladness, to be at one with each other in silent unspeakable memories?

George Eliot

In his younger days a man dreams of possessing the heart of the woman whom he loves; later, the feeling that he possesses the heart of a woman may be enough to make him fall in love with her.

Marcel Proust

To fear love is to fear life.

Bertrand Russell

The greatest happiness of life is the conviction that we are loved—loved for ourselves or, rather, loved in spite of ourselves.

Victor Hugo

Feeling is the language of love
we feel before we speak, and our
feelings speak volumes.

Love is the triumph of imagination over intelligence.

H. L. Mencken

Love is energy of life.

Robert Browning

To love is to be vulnerable.

C. S. Lewis

Love is that condition in which the happiness of another person is essential to your own.

Robert A. Heinlein

There is no placebo for love—the power of love is beyond compare.

Friendship may, and often does, grow into love, but love never subsides into friendship.

Lord Byron

Lord, make me an instrument of Your peace!
Where there is hatred let me sow love.

Saint Francis of Assisi

Love is something eternal; the aspect may change, but not the essence.

Vincent Van Gogh

One may sow a million
seeds of love but only one
will thrive and have meaning.

Love produces a certain flowering
of the whole personality which
nothing else can possibly achieve.

Love is the child of freedom —
it can never be dominated.

He who is devoid of the power to
forgive is devoid of the power to love.
Martin Luther King

In those whom I like, I can find no
common denominator; in those whom
I love, I can: they all make me laugh.
W. H. Auden

This was love at first sight, love everlasting: a feeling unknown, unhoped for, unexpected—in so far as it could be a matter of conscious awareness; it took entire possession of him, and he understood, with joyous amazement, that this was for life.

Thomas Mann

The person in love is not the person we become. When we fall in love, we become who we already are.

Joy is a net of love that captures souls.

Mother Teresa

Love is what happens to men and women who don't know each other.

W. Somerset Maugham

Life is to be fortified by many friendships. To love and to be loved is the greatest happiness of existence.

Sydney Smith

If love were what the rose is,
And I were like the leaf,
Our lives would grow together
In sad or singing weather.

Algernon Swinburne

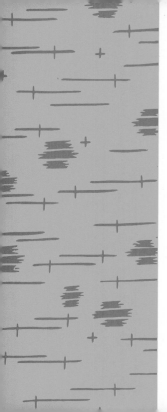

Love is the
reward of love.

Schiller

Grow old along
with me, the best
is yet to be.

Robert Browning

Where there is love
there is life.

Mahatma Gandhi

Spread love everywhere you go: first of all in your own home. Give love to your children, to a wife or husband, to a nextdoor neighbor.

Mother Teresa

You yourself, as much as anybody in the entire universe, deserve your love and affection.

Buddha

Tell me who admires and loves you, and I will tell you who you are.

Charles Augustin Sainte-Beuve

It is only with the heart that one can see rightly; what is essential is invisible to the eye.

Antoine de Saint-Exupéry

Those that go searching for love only make manifest their own lovelessness, and the loveless never find love, only the loving find love, and they never have to seek for it.

D. H. Lawrence

Love sought is good, but given unsought is better.

William Shakespeare

Love is a canvas furnished
by nature and embroidered
by imagination.

Voltaire

**Love is composed of a single
soul inhabiting two bodies.**

Aristotle

Everything that
deceives also
enchants.

Plato

Don't forget to love
yourself.

Søren Kierkegaard

Love is the exchange of two
fantasies and the contact
of two skins.

Sébastien-Roch Nicolas Chamfort

Being deeply loved by
someone gives you
strength, while loving
someone deeply gives
you courage.

Lao-tzu

Wicked men obey from fear;
good men, from love.

Aristotle

My bounty is as boundless as the sea,
My love as deep; the more I give to thee
The more I have, for both are infinite.

William Shakespeare

Gravitation is not responsible
for people falling in love.

Albert Einstein

That farewell kiss which
resembles greeting; that last
glance of love which becomes
the sharpest pang of sorrow.

George Eliot

We know the truth not only by
reason but by the heart.

Blaise Pascal

Love is first friendship
and then commitment.

Jacques Pierre Ribault

At the touch of love
everyone becomes a poet.

Plato

To love and be loved is to find
paradise on earth.

Is love
merely
an act of
endless
forgiveness,
a tender
look which
becomes a
habit ?

Love is a smoke made with
the fume of sighs.

> William Shakespeare

Love will find a way through
paths where wolves fear to prey.

> Lord Byron

She who has never loved
has never lived.

> John Gay

True love is eternal, infinite, and always like itself. It is equal and pure, without violent demonstrations: it is seen with white hairs and is always young in the heart.

Honoré de Balzac

Love is a hole in the heart.

Ben Hecht

There is no disguise which can hide
love for long where it exists, or simulate
it where it does not.

François, Duc de La Rochefoucauld

All love that has not friendship for its base
is like a mansion built upon the sand.

Ella Wheeler Wilcox

Love is a disease
which fills you with a
desire to be desired.

Henri de Toulouse-Lautrec

When we love someone or something, we admire with the heart.
When we admire something or someone, we love with the mind.

Kindness in words creates confidence.
Kindness in thinking creates profoundness.
Kindness in giving creates love.

Lao-tzu

When we are in love we often doubt that which we most believe.
François, Duc de La Rochefoucauld

The best portion of
a good man's life is
his little, nameless,
unremembered
acts of kindness
and of love.

William Wordsworth

Anything will give up its secrets if you love it enough. Not only have I found that when I talk to the little flower or to the little peanut they will give up their secrets, but I have found that when I silently commune with people they give up their secrets also —if you love them enough.

George Washington Carver

True love grows by sacrifice, and the more thoroughly the soul rejects natural satisfaction the stronger and more detached its tenderness becomes.

Saint Theresa of Lisieux

Those who love us provide a resting place, as we find rest in those we love.

We don't love to be loved—
we love to love.

The pleasure of love is in the loving; and there is more joy in the passion one feels than in that which one inspires.

François, Duc de La Rochefoucauld

True love is bestowed as a gift. It is given freely, willingly, and unconditionally.

Real love begins where nothing
is expected in return.

Antoine de Saint-Exupéry

Give all to love; obey thy heart.

Ralph Waldo Emerson

Love endures when the lovers
love many things together
and not merely each other.

Walter Lippmann

We are not the same persons this
year as last; nor are those we love.
It is a happy chance if we, changing,
continue to love a changed person.

W. Somerset Maugham

The love of a new day is a virgin
love.

Love in its essence is spiritual fire.

Emanuel Swedenborg

If we judge of love by its usual effects, it resembles hatred more than friendship.

François, Duc de La Rochefoucauld

Because of a great love, one is courageous.

Lao-tzu

The motto of chivalry is also the motto of wisdom; to serve all, but love only one.

Honoré de Balzac

What does love look like? It has the hands to help others. It has the feet to hasten to the poor and needy. It has eyes to see misery and want. It has the ears to hear the sighs and sorrows of men. That is what love looks like.

Saint Augustine

To live is like to love—all reason is against it, and all healthy instinct for it.

Samuel Butler

A joyful heart is the inevitable result of a heart burning with love.

Mother Teresa

There is no remedy for love but to love more.

Henry David Thoreau

It is impossible to love and to be wise.

Francis Bacon

It is wrong to think that love comes from long companionship and persevering courtship. Love is the offspring of spiritual affinity and unless that affinity is created in a moment, it will not be created for years or even generations.

Kahlil Gibran

He who is in love is wise and is becoming wiser, sees newly every time he looks at the object beloved, drawing from it with his eyes and his mind those virtues it possesses.

Ralph Waldo Emerson

Love is not complex or mystical. It is an everyday occurrence and therefore should not be treated as some abstract thing beyond our reach.

Nothing is sweeter than Eros. All
delights hold second place—I spit
out from my mouth even honey.

                                        Nossis

Love is a wound within the body
that has no outward sign.

                            Marie de France

Very difficult is this discipline of love.

Love is like a beautiful flower which I may not touch, but whose fragrance makes the garden a place of delight just the same.

Helen Keller

I fell in love with her courage, her sincerity, and her flaming self-respect, and it's these things I'd believe in even if the whole world indulged in wild suspicions that she wasn't all she should be. I love her and that's the beginning of everything.

F. Scott Fitzgerald

Those who love liberty love
others. Those who love
power love only themselves.

Love is the question
and love is the answer.

A lover without indiscretion
is no lover at all.

Thomas Hardy

Skies, trees, hills, snow, rain, and winds are dearer to me than all the wonders of the human heart. To understand and to love nature, one only needs a willing and trusting heart, but it takes a brave heart to understand and love human beings.

Anaïs Nin

A lawful kiss is never worth a stolen one.

Guy de Maupassant

A pity beyond all
telling is hid in the
heart of love.
W. B. Yeats

Absence is to love
what wind is to fire;
it extinguishes the
small, it inflames
the great.
Christopher Marlowe

Lovers' thoughts have wings.

Beauty is not in the face;
beauty is a light in the heart.

Kahlil Gibran

All are beautiful who are loved.

Beauty provokes thieves sooner than gold.

William Shakespeare

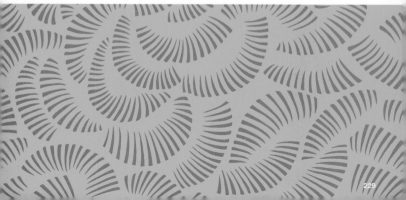

Eyes of most
unholy blue!

Thomas More

Beloved, all that is harsh and difficult I want for myself, and all that is gentle and sweet for thee.

San Juan de la Cruz

Come live with me and be my love,
And we will some new pleasures prove
Of golden sands, and crystal brooks,
With silken lines, and silver hooks.

John Donne

Some people say there are plenty of fish in the sea, until you find love— then there is only one.

In the confusion we stay with each other, happy to be together, speaking without uttering a single word.

Walt Whitman

It is love, not reason, that is stronger than death.

Thomas Mann

It is with true love as it is with ghosts; everyone talks about it, but few have seen it.

François, Duc de La Rochefoucauld

Love is the flower of life, and
blossoms unexpectedly and
without law, and must be
plucked where it is found,
and enjoyed for the brief hour
of its duration.

D. H. Lawrence

Life is the flower for which
love is the honey.

Victor Hugo

The mind has a thousand eyes,
And the heart but one;
Yet the light of a whole life dies,
When love is done.

F. W. Bourdillon

Paradise was made for tender
hearts; hell, for loveless hearts.

Voltaire

I am two fools,
I know, for loving,
and for saying so
in whining poetry.

John Donne

Real beauty lies in the spiritual accord
that is called love which can exist
between a man and a woman.

Kahlil Gibran

We are shaped and
fashioned by what we love.

Openness and honesty will
bring us the love we deserve.

Love keeps the cold out better
than a cloak.

Henry Wadsworth Longfellow

Who, being loved, is poor?
Oscar Wilde

Love can sometimes be magic. But magic can sometimes just be an illusion.

Deceive the eyes, perhaps, but never the heart.

God loves each of us as if there were only one of us.

Saint Augustine

Love and you
shall be loved.

Ralph Waldo Emerson

Is it Love?

Love—though invisible, unmeasurable, and often unattainable—is the most formidable force known to man.

It is one love to want only good for another person and quite another love to want that person.

Love is what you are.

Over centuries man has learned
to breathe air, walk upright, and to
communicate, but he hasn't yet grasped
the vital thing, which is that in order not to
perish he must learn to love.

Most agree that they are only prepared
to love so long as it doesn't involve any
personal risk.

Love can provide greater bliss than any wealth or possession, and is capable of transforming a person's entire being in an instant.

What greater satisfaction than those early days of new love when two people walk through life oblivious to everything else?

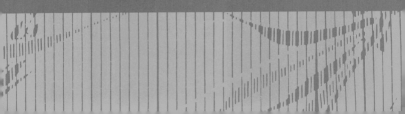

The only real enemy of true love
is life itself.

The good will obey through love.
The wicked only obey through fear.

Love is an envelope containing
jealousy, suspicion, anger,
and fear.

What is a face
without love?

We are never so
defenseless against
suffering as when
we love, never so
forlornly unhappy
as when we have
lost our love object
or its love.

Sigmund Freud

**You will know love
only when you find it.**

Some go through life feeling
shame for a lack of talent
when they should know this—
it is enough to have common
sense and love.

**Oh love — the wildest woe,
the sweetest joy.**

Love is more than merely a way
of getting someone to call you
"darling" after sex.

When it is your time,
love will find you.

Love is the river of life.

Love is patient and kind; love
is not jealous or boastful;
it is not arrogant or rude.

I Corinthians

Love seeketh not itself to please,
Nor for itself hath any care,
But for another gives its ease,
And builds a Heaven in Hell's despair.
William Blake

We curious creatures called mankind will willingly trade a month of honey for a lifetime of vinegar.

Experience counts for nothing in love—for how many times do the heartbroken avoid newfound love?

There is no happy ending for true love, for true love will never end.

Who, that would fall in love,
can predict how hard a master
their love will be.

**What is that feeling?
It is all the little
emptiness of love!**

If we hold on to
hate, anger, pain,
and hurt, love
will either pass
us by or we
will not have
the energy for it.

Is it delirium or could
it be love?

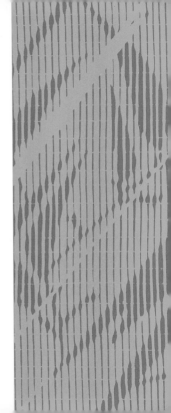

It is clear to see in this world that there are those who are in love with their lovers and those who are in love only with love.

While it is possible to give without loving, it is quite impossible to love without giving.

Who is it that will love when not loved back?

Love feels no burden.

Once your passion is confirmed, it is impossible to lay it aside.

It is far better to have loved a short person than never to have loved a tall!

Love that is incapable of loving the unlovable is not real love.

Man's discovery of fire is relived every day at that moment when two people fall in love.

Love is not to be hidden away. Share it with your friends—fill their lives with cheer and romance, thrill their hearts — and they too shall be made happy by your love.

The greatest waste one can leave behind in life is the love that has not been given.

Love itself costs nothing — unlike the accessories that accompany it.

Each touch, each kiss, each embrace is a star in love's universe.

Love lies waiting at the edge of each tear.

Love can be a tyrant, it spares no one.

If love is a fire, will it warm your hearth or will it burn down your house?

It is impossible to love another without undertaking some fragment of their destiny.

How often do we tell our partner: "I love you, not for what you are, but for what I am when I am with you"?

Love is able to tame even the wildest spirit, and often turns the tamest spirit wild.

The secret of a long and happy life is to do everything you do with love in your heart.

Are we taught to love? We tend to love only what we can understand, and we can only understand that which we are taught.

The magic of first love is our blissful ignorance that it can never end.

What is time or climate to love? Love has no seasons or boundaries.

Some avoid love altogether, choosing to see it as a universe of complex emotions, with each star representing another expense.

Love is life.

The wise are blinded by love, and fools become enlightened.

The pain of love and the pain of being alive are one and the same.

Everybody loves a lover.

It is wrong to believe that you will be loved for who you are. You will be loved for how you make people feel.

Those who fall in love with themselves have no rivals.

It is odd how love tends
to make us laugh too loud
and talk too much.

The simple rule in life is this:
love while you are able to love.

Love is the perfect solution to
the puzzle of human existence.

Whenever you are confronted with an opponent, conquer him with love.

Mahatma Gandhi

They say that love is often blind. It is not so—indeed, love sees more and, because of this, it often chooses to see less.

What business is it of yours if I love you?

Forcing love is about as easy a task as the alchemist struggling to create gold.

There are as many reasons not to fall in love as there are for doing so.

If you are capable of love, then you are truly alive.

Hiding love is
about as easy as
hiding hiccups.

Love becomes meaningless when we
try to embrace everything equally with it.

Love ripens, like fruit,
and goes bad if not consumed.

Love is a vital equation
in the mathematics of life.

Love is the key which opens
the gates of happiness.

Lovers are nature's fools.

Love is everything that it's cracked up to be. That's why people are so cynical about it.

One can never forget the feeling of being in love.

Many talk about finding true love, but how many have found it?

When you are able to place your happiness in the happiness of another, then you will know love.

It is easier to love those who admire us than those we admire.

What good are tears of love when they cannot be seen?

Love is as simple and as difficult as this:
love one another and you will be happy.

Who can resist seeing themselves in
the mirror of their lover's eyes—who
can ever be the same after that?

Love is inseparable from knowledge.

Love is a sexier extension of liking
somebody.

The one treasure we can take with us to the grave is the love we have treasured in this life.

As friends we enjoy each other on a platform of equality, while love thrives on opposites and extremes.

A love affair with knowledge
will never end in heartbreak.

**Love means the body, the
soul, the life, the entire being.**

When we are in a state of love,
nothing else can possibly hurt us.

**Love is found in the most
unexpected places.**

Love cures—the ones
who give it, and the ones
who receive it.

**Despite the old adage
that you can't buy love, the
world is filled to the brim
with people who are paying
heavily because of it.**

What is that feeling that passes
between two lovers when they touch?

Love is like a wild rose,
beautiful and delicate,
but handle it wrongly
and you will feel a thorn.

If any person wishes to be idle,
let them fall in love.

Love laughs at locksmiths.

Anyone that plants trees loves others besides himself.

Like is when one kisses and the other offers a cheek. Love is when both offer kisses.

Love is like the measles: all the worse when it comes late.

Love is what is left in a relationship after all the selfishness is taken out.

There is only one happiness in life—to love and to be loved in return.

If you wish to be loved, you must be worthy of love. To be worthy of love, you must love!

Love produces a certain flowering of the whole personality which nothing else can achieve.

Love and stoplights can be cruel.

Love sought is good,
but given unsought is better.

Reason and love keep little
company together.

Want of love is an emptiness
that robs the joy from life.

All is fair in love and war.

Love is not about counting the years—
it's about making the years count.

One word frees us
of all the weight
and pain of life;
that word is love.

Sophocles

There is little a person will not dare
when strong affection stirs the spirit.

To fall in love is easy, even to
remain in it is not difficult.

Those who feel love receive
a glimpse of heaven.

Love is a flame — it can either
light the way to happiness,
or burn your fingers.

A life without
love in it is
like a heap of
cold ashes in a
hearth, the fire
dead, all warmth
and laughter
gone, and no
more light.

Love is everything. It is the key to life, and its influences are those that move the world.

Be yourself. That is the quickest route to love.

Love is the passion of one being for another in the hope of being loved in return.

How can you hope to fall in love with somebody else if you cannot love yourself?

Live for love, by all means, but place your love wisely.

They say that love is blind. If that is so, why is so much of it done in the dark?

Once you have learned to love, you
will have learned to live.

Without love you can do nothing—with
love there is nothing you cannot do.

Lovers are two people with
one heart between them.

The object of love is to serve,
not to win.

The moment one attempts
to become sensible
about love, one becomes
incapable of love.

In a relationship, often
the three words needed
to hold it together are not
"I love you,"
but "I am sorry."

You don't just feel love,
you do love,
act love,
live love.

Love and
Kisses

Kisses that are
easily obtained
are easily forgotten.

Love dictates the message
which is delivered by a kiss.
One kiss is all it takes to
breach the distance between
friendship and love.

Life is a gift of nature,
love is a gift of life,
kisses are the gift of love.

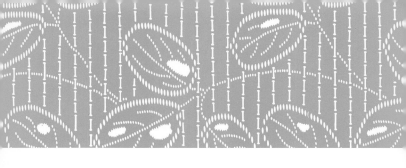

Give me a kiss, and to that kiss a score;
Then to that twenty, add a hundred more:
A thousand to that hundred: so kiss on,
To make that thousand up a million.
Treble that million, and when that is done,
Let's kiss afresh, as when we first begun.

Robert Herrick

Love is a sudden revelation; each kiss is a new discovery.

Kissing is like drinking salted water— as you drink, your thirst increases.

Send some kisses to someone you know who likes them.

Love is like
a butterfly.
It goes
where it
pleases,
alighting
with a kiss,
pleasing all
who see it.

The lips are like bees and kisses are pollen,
Love is honey—sweet to the soul.

Through kisses, love grows.

A kiss is sweetened by passion
and sanctified by affection.

Each man kills the thing he loves—
with a bitter look, with a flattering
word, with a sword, or with a kiss.

A kiss is the currency of love.

Sex is a momentary itch.

A loving kiss never lets you go.

No words are necessary between two loving hearts.

A kiss is understood
in any language.

**Take and return
each kiss with love.**

A kiss given in love takes
the breath away, and in
that silence a thousand
things are unsaid.

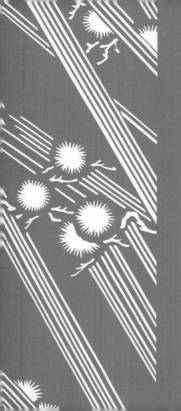

Even strangers can't avoid falling in love with those that kiss them. Who could help but love the stranger that gave you the kiss of life?

The human heart feels things our eyes cannot see, and a kiss speaks the words we dare not say.

The kiss is a sweet discovery of oneself after a long search.

The most eloquent silence must surely be that of two mouths meeting in a kiss.

The conversation between lovers is confusing to everyone but them — they should just kiss; then everyone could understand.

There are two ways of spreading our light—we can either be like the candle or like the mirror that reflects it.

Kisses are curious things. They are the punctuation marks of a relationship.

To the world you may just be someone, but to someone you may be the whole world.

Wait for the one you love, not the one who found you first.

Kissing someone is the only true adventure—everything hinges on that moment.

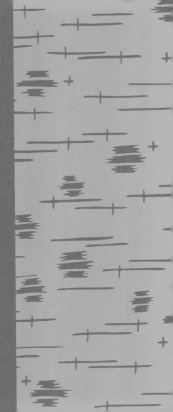

You don't get to choose to fall in love.
You just fall.

You may forget the face of
someone you once loved,
but you'll always remember their kiss.

Be careful when you fall in love:
you might fall and keep falling
for an entire lifetime.

When you kiss someone, you enter
into a dialogue between two souls.

You can't fake kissing.

How deep is our love?
How deep is the ocean?

When we fall in love, it is reassuring to know that we are not the only ones who feel this way.

When we fall out of love, it is reassuring to know that we are not the only ones who feel this way.

Hiding the love we feel for somebody is like trying to hide an elephant.

Love while you
are able to love.

Never mock love, for you
too might fall victim to it.

Love will attempt to lead
you in one direction while
understanding lures you
the other way. Let yourself
be led by love.

**A kiss
is a kiss
is a kiss.**

**He who is not
impatient is not
in love.**

There is a
kiss for every
occasion.

Love is shelter, come
in from the rain.

Kisses are
lighthouses for
vessels lost in
the fog on the
ocean of love.

Love is the big fish,
kisses are the bait.

When you're in love, kisses
light the sky like fireworks.

Once you have learned to love
you will have learned to live.

Love is not just a feeling, but
an everlasting commitment
to each other.

Love is a love-hate relationship: you love to hate the one who loves the one you hate to love.

Tears are like kisses. Both come from the heart when there are words you just can't say.

When you have nothing left but love, then for the first time you become aware that love is enough.

A kiss can change the world.

When you say
"I love you,"
mean it.
When you kiss,
mean it.

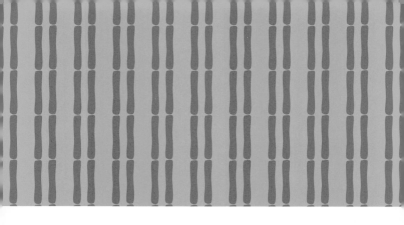

Sad mouths can have
smiles kissed into them.

Friends are kisses blown
to us by angels.

Believe in love at first kiss.

Anyone who can describe a kiss is simply not giving their kissing the attention that it deserves!

Is it a kiss hello, or a kiss goodbye?

Wait a lifetime to get to know a person
better before you kiss them, or kiss them
and get to know them immediately.

There is the unexpected kiss, and then
there is the kiss that arrives sooner
than you thought it would.

Kisses are jumper cables for the heart.

Should we trust anyone who doesn't close their eyes when they kiss? Should we trust anyone who does close their eyes when they kiss? In one case they might be looking at your friend while they kiss you, in the other case they might be dreaming of your friend while they kiss you. The best solution is to kiss looking into each other's eyes!

When parting with a kiss, consider how lucky you are to have known someone so difficult to say goodbye to.

Choose to love, and you will choose to live happily ever after.

If you love something, you must respect its freedom.

In the end, all things surrender to feeling.

A kiss brings us closer than
words ever can.

We can speak of love, but
only by being in love can
we truly know love.

If in doubt, kiss.

The loves that survive
the longest are those
that didn't begin with
finding the perfect person.

Every kiss of love feels like the first.

Distance makes the heart grow fonder — only sometimes not for the distant person.

Kisses are the reward of love.

What the majority
call madness the
smitten call love.

True love is a
force of nature.

If you are going to give a kiss, make it a kiss worth giving.

Don't enter into a love affair with the fear that it will end.

It is curious that the symptoms of love are also the symptoms of physical, and mental, illness.

We never laugh, or cry, as much as when we are in love.

You might have played footsie, but have you tried playing heartsie?

You know when you have found your love because the smile in your heart will be bigger than the smile on your face.

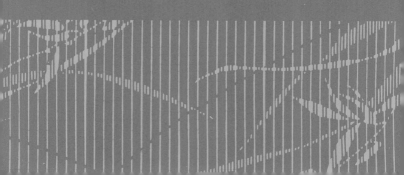

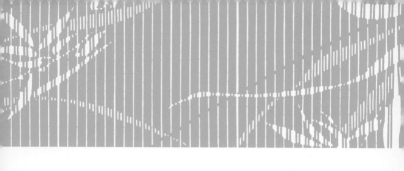

Don't let a kiss make a fool of you—
follow your head *and* your heart.

**Love fills the heart with joy,
fills togetherness with fun,
and fills partings with sweet sorrow.**

Trip over love and you can get up—fall in love and you fall forever.

Love is not about changing people to fit our own image; it is about letting them be themselves.

Love is the dew that falls on both nettles and petals.

Kisses are
sweet as
spring rain.

We do not judge the people we love.

A kiss underlines the words "I love you."

A kiss is worth nothing if you keep it to yourself. Give it away and its value soars.

Sometimes, the love we are looking for is right in front of us, too close for the eyes to see. Let your heart do the searching.

One thing is for certain: if it's not mutual love, it's not really love.

There is no disguise which can hide love for long where it exists, or simulate it where it does not.

François, Duc de La Rochefoucauld

A kiss is something you cannot give without taking, and cannot take without giving.

Nothing breaks the silence like a kiss.

The first kiss of love is sweeter than honey.

Some people think it's holding on that makes us strong—sometimes it all comes down to letting go.

**Sometimes we see things
not as they are but as we are.
Love brings a special kind
of understanding.**

One kiss is never enough.

If you would be kissed, kiss.

Only the brave can exhibit love.

Those who have experienced true love can never really be alone.

A kiss can't lie.

False love is a thousand times worse than nothing.

No two kisses are the same— there are as many different kisses as there are lovers to give them.

The first kiss of love is a revelation.

Be happy with your love. Don't keep looking over your shoulder to see if there is anything better coming along.

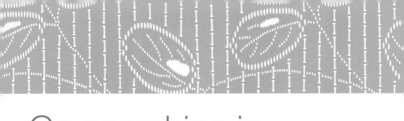

Go searching in
expectation of what
love will give you, and
you will never find it.
Open your heart and be
prepared only to give,
and love will find you.

There is nowhere to hide from love.

The sweetest gift is a kiss freely given.

Love is its own reward.

You aren't wealthy until you have something money can't buy.

Is it better to be kissed or to kiss?

A kiss lives for a moment on the lips, but for a lifetime in the heart.

A kiss has the healing power to mend a broken heart.

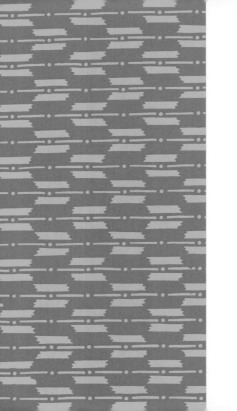

It is said that
love starts
with a kiss
and ends
with a tear.

A kiss
has the
power to
change
a life.

Has anyone ever measured how much love a heart can hold?

Idolizing is when you put someone on a pedestal; true love is when you put someone on a pedestal but are prepared to catch them if they fall.

We all want to fall in love because it is through love that we feel alive.

You cannot be taught how to kiss; leave it to instinct.

A kiss is the breeze that fans the flames of love.

**Nothing can heighten
the senses like love.**

The memory of a kiss never dies. It
remains in the heart as fresh and as
sweet as the moment it was given.

A kiss should always be received in the spirit with which it is given.

Self-Love

Most people would rather give than get affection.

We can control our emotions with no greater ease than we can control the weather.

Love is an emotion that a person always feels for their pet and sometimes for a human.

Affection is a delicacy whose recipe consists of a mixture of admiration seasoned with a liberal sprinkling of pity.

Why are so many so
afraid of showing affection?
Love often
takes the form of a few
kind, well-timed words,
and these can provide
infinitely more pleasure
than any purchased
gift or present.

When does like become love? When does a life become worth living?

Love has a curious way of making each lover strive to make the other entirely happy and, should that fail, then they resort to tactics designed to make the other feel entirely wretched.

Greater hate hath no person for another than the other side of love.

Love is a bargain that it takes two to strike.

Love is
Agreeable, **B**ountiful,
Constant, **D**utiful,
Easy, **F**aithful,
Gallant, **H**onorable,
Ingenious, **J**ust,
Kind, **L**oyal **M**ild,
Noble, **O**fficious,
Prudent, **Q**uiet,
Rich, **S**ecret, **T**rue,
Unique, **V**aliant,
Wise; **X** = kiss, **Y**oung
at heart,
and **Z**ealous.

Love won too easily is often not valued as highly as that which has been fought for.

Age cannot wither her,
nor custom stale her infinite variety.
Other women cloy the appetites
they feed, but she makes hungry
where most she satisfies.

William Shakespeare

The pressure is upon us in life to accept the belief that love is dead once sexual passion has run its course, but for many it is not until sex has died out that they can really begin to love.

We strive to obtain the love that is beyond our grasp, believing that it cannot be worth having if we already have it.

Love is the greatest investment, if you dare to take the risk.

The greatest and best-felt intimacy is the moment of mutual embarrassment—what closer moment can there be between two people than when each knows full well what the other feels?

The important thing to realize about romantic love is that it almost always begins so wonderfully that it can only be followed by an uncertain term of sadness and impossibility.

To truly love, you must have an innocent heart.

And what's romance? Usually, a nice little tale where you have everything As You Like It, where rain never wets your jacket, and gnats never bite your nose, and it's always daisy-time.

D. H. Lawrence

Time, not intensity, is the greatest test of love.

Odd, is it not, how a torrid sexual affair can, by the addition of romance, become something altogether different and entirely pardonable.

No love strikes so hard, or tastes so sweet, as first love.

Self-love is too often viewed as a negative trait. But consider this: if a person is unable to love themself, then how can they possibly be any good at loving anybody else?

Please yourself.

The beginning of losing one's misery comes through the resolution to get to know oneself. Once done, you can begin to create room in your life for other things and people who will bring joy into your life.

Love is the coming-together of two one-winged angels.

We can be whatever age we like in our own minds, so why do we allow ourselves to be bothered by other people who would make us out to be too old for love?

There is not one wise man in twenty that will praise himself.

William Shakespeare

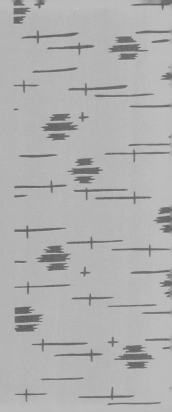

For most of us the debate about whether, given the choice, we'd rather have riches or good looks begins and ends in front of the bathroom mirror.

Self-love is the most arrogant form of love. It persuades us that our faults escape the notice of others while they remain in full view to ourselves.

The snow goose need not bathe to make itself white. Neither need you do anything but be yourself.

Lao-tzu

Until we are able to accept ourselves as we are, we will remain undeserving to ourselves and we will never move forward.

The greatest lie detector in the world is the bathroom mirror.

In a mirror, look yourself fully in the eyes and tell yourself you did the best you could.

None will love those they fear.

Love is the only true living adventure.

Attempting to fall in love, or not to fall in love, is like trying to predict when and where a lightning bolt will strike.

The longest relationship you're going to have in this life is with yourself, so you should make certain that you like yourself or you'll go nowhere.

It's a well-known fact that when we feel good about ourselves others feel good about us.

You are your own worst enemy, and your greatest friend.

**It is easier to have a relationship
with a thousand people than it is
to have one with yourself.**

Your Self sits in the car
The body is the car
The intellect is the driver
And the mind is the steering wheel.

after Upanishads

**The most unrequited form
of love is self-love.**

For some, the highest level of sexual excitement is in a solo relationship.

A relationship can be seen to be working when you pass two people arguing and holding hands.

For most, it is the things they have in common that makes their relationships enjoyable, but it is the subtle differences that give it spice.

Be a bit selfish if you want your relationship to work.

To love requires a sense of humor.

My attachment has neither the blindness of the beginning, nor the microscopic accuracy of the close of such liaisons.

Lord Byron

To love is to be vulnerable—it leaves us open to the possibility of a broken heart.

The only way never to suffer through love is never to love.

Our first and last love is self-love.

When love turns bad, it is like watching the Sugar Plum Fairy turn into a machete-wielding terrorist.

How can it be possible to be wise and in love? They are a total contradiction and are therefore quite impossible to do at the same time.

For those who may be tempted to lie to gain another's heart, remember that all the crowd love the illusion, not the illusionist.

Where there is greatness,
there is a soul fueled by love.

In love the main paradox is that two
beings become one yet remain two.
There is no such paradox in self-love.

You cannot get rid of love. The more
you try to give it away, the more it
will come back to you.

Mother Teresa said that we
should spread love everywhere
we go—starting in our own house.

When we look back from the high hill of our old age to the life we have led, we will find that many of the moments we felt really alive were the ones where we pleased only ourselves.

If love is the child of illusion, then it is almost certainly the parent of disillusion.

Love can make us or break us.

Love is what we make of it.

Love is the greatest gift we can
ever give, and that is the gift of ourself.

Miracles are the offspring of love.

I cannot point you in the direction of love
while you remain determined to search
for it abroad, but I can tell you that your
search must begin closer to home.

Do not be selfish with your love; love thrives on generosity.

Let no one ever come to you without leaving better and happier. Be the living expression of God's kindness; kindness in your face, kindness in your eyes, kindness in your smile, kindness in your warm greeting.

Mother Teresa

Apart from anything else, love
keeps the heart busy.

Love those who love you.

Love given through pity is
no love at all.

Love is the path through the darkness
where wolves fear to prey.

The greatest thief of joy is
the emptiness created
through want of love.

A woman's love is much rarer than a man's, for women will love much and far more rarely than a man, while a man will love little and often.

Love is about two people living together who cannot live without each other for the rest of their lives, each hoping to die the day before the other so they never have to live without them.

You will never get left on the shelf if you love yourself.

**At first I thought you caught my eye,
then as time passed I realized that
my first glance fell on your heart.**

My friend, let's not think of tomorrow, but
let's enjoy this fleeting moment of life.

Omar Khayyám

**Love is there to catch us when we
fall; it is also there to trip us up.**

There is no person alive who is worth
our tears. For anyone that we feel might
be would never drive us to crying!

Love gives us the strength to lighten
the burden of others and ourselves.

**No sooner met but they looked;
no sooner looked but they loved;
no sooner loved but they sighed;
no sooner sighed
but they asked one another the reason;
no sooner knew the reason
but they sought the remedy.**

William Shakespeare

What words are needed
between two loving hearts?

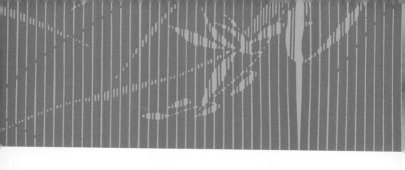

What surprise can possibly rival
the magical effect that comes from
discovering we are loved?

**No matter how old we are, dreams
of love will keep us young.**

Who has ever been betrayed
by real love?

Love is that place where heaven and hell coexist.

Those of us who have loved and been loved will always love and be loved, even though over time our memories may fade from our minds. What remains in our heart will live forever.

A kiss is a secret told to the mouth instead of to the ear.

The swiftest bridge that was ever built is the one that connects friendship and love, for it is constructed in a moment.

Be your own best friend.

Outside may be stormy
but together we are
a safe
we.

Sweeter than all the pleasures
in this life are the pains of love.

Those who insist upon tearing
through life in search of the perfect
lover must learn that there is no such
thing. Such time spent would be
better employed creating perfect love.

Love is all or nothing.

There is no happiness as intense
as that of two lovers, nor misery
as abject as that of one.

Reason is the enemy of love.

Do not choose the first person who comes along—practice first and find true love later.

Love's effect upon free men is to compel them to tear through life in a frantic quest to discover someone to worship.

The eye can lie.

Love is to couples what the flowers are to spring.

Strength is as much about letting go as it is about holding on.

We go through life seeing things not as they are but as we are, and love is the only lens available to straighten out our vision of the world and offer some hope of understanding.

The earth grows colder without love.

A kiss of love should be taken, but don't forget to return it.

The course of true love
never did run smooth.

William Shakespeare

The first duty of love is to listen.

The heart has its reasons,
whereof reason knows nothing.

Our bodies may age,
our memories may wither,
but the heart has no wrinkles.

You will not be
judged by how
much you love,
but by how
much you are
loved by others.

The greatest act of self-discovery often happens with a kiss.

The love of beauty in all its forms is the greatest gift of all.

Can there be any experience greater than surrendering our heart?

Stand still and listen to love.

You may run the entire world over looking for the person of your dreams, but lovers are in each other all along.

Don't ever frown —
you never know
who's falling in love
with your smile.

Love reduces the entire universe to a single being, and then expands that person to the stature of a living god.

Have you ever been kissed by a glance?

The supreme happiness of life is the conviction that we are loved, and that we are worthy of that love.

Love is perhaps the only glimpse
of heaven we shall ever get.

Love is the candle that lights
our way, and we are the mirror
that reflects it.

There is no fear in love; but
perfect love casteth out fear:
because fear hath torment.
He that feareth is not made
perfect in love.

John 4:18

There is no protection against love.

This is the true measure of love:
when we believe that we alone can love,
that no one could ever
have loved so before us,
and that no one will ever love
in the same way after us.

Goethe

Seek no other reward than love itself.

Those who live
for love
live.

Divine
Love

We know we're in love when we are
unable to explain how we are in love.

Love is beauty and
love is the beauty of the soul,
for love grows within us.

Love is the essence of God.

Divine love comes to those prepared to share what they have with those who have little or nothing — and that includes love, so the more love we feel, the more love we can share.

Everything that we understand, we understand only because we love.

Love alone is capable of uniting living beings, joining them by what is deepest within them.

We can only realize
the true depth of
our love at the
hour of separation.

When our love is
true, our lover's
hand becomes
our own, and we
see the world
through their eyes.

All life before
love is but a
preparation
for love.

When the one man loves the one woman, and the one woman loves the one man, the very angels leave heaven and come sit in that house and sing for joy.

Brahma

Love is a glimpse of heaven.

Only when the spirit is pure are we truly ready to love.

We can call for divine
assistance whenever
we need help—all
we need to do is
open ourselves for it.

Cast aside all cynicism
if you want to love.

Who will know heaven
who has not known love?

Divine love is there for those who go out
of their way to try to make others happy.

**As we are healed
so we will learn to love
and learn to heal others.**

Lovers recognize the beauty
of the soul.

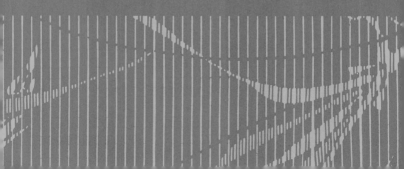

The more love you give each day, the more love you will receive.

All who share love are never alone, but are part of one single family united by love.

Do not confuse love with the experience of being in love—love remains even after the other has faded.

Who seeks love through lies? It is better to be hated for telling the truth than adored for being something you're not.

A very small degree of hope is sufficient to bring about the birth of love.

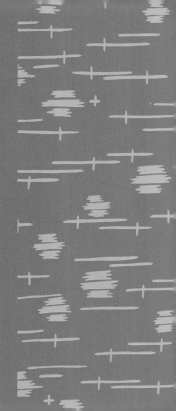

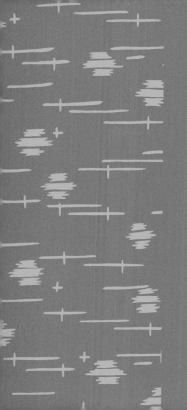

There is only
one remedy for
lovesickness—
love even more.

The beauty of
love is this: it never
fades away,
it comes to us in
a moment, and
stays with us
forever. Unlike
lust, it never dies.

Love is the very reason we are here. It is the greatest and perhaps the only real truth there is. So why is it such a difficult word for us to use?

It is impossible for love and suspicion to dwell together.

Those things we love become part of us.

Why is the loneliness felt at the end of a love affair so much worse than that felt before the love affair began?

Didn't you know that people hide love like a flower too precious to be picked?

Wu Ti

What makes a life are those small, unremembered acts of kindness and love.

In life, one has
more chance
of holding
an ocean
in the palm
of the hand
than avoiding
falling in love.

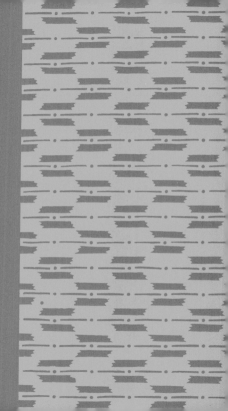

Love is more than Valentines.

It suddenly strikes you that you are
no longer alone in this world, all fear
vanishes and you realize that love has
come to stay.

It is impossible to find your own
romance in someone else's love story.

Love guards the roses of thy lips
And flies about them like a bee;
If I approach he forward skips,
And if I kiss he stingeth me.

Thomas Lodge

I love you, not for what you are, but for what you are now that I love you, and for what you make me.

True love creates an "us" without destroying a "me."

The only love that has value is the love we give away.

Who travels for love
finds a thousand miles
not longer than one.

Japanese proverb

Life is a journey, and love is
what makes it all worthwhile.

If you want to look at it from a
different angle, even unrequited
love is a form of love.

Know that love is here and now.

Love is the most
important thing
in our lives.

Love creates
our fondest
memories.
Love is the
foundation of
our dreams.

In one lifetime you can fritter away a fortune but you cannot fritter away love.

Love is a seed that can flourish in even the most unlikely of places.

There is no award for being in love.
Love is the reward.

Being truly in love is being able to feel that
we are the existence of another person.

There will always be truth between
those who share love for each other.

It is difficult for some
people to accept
that love is a choice.

Having the capacity to love is not the same as having the ability to love.

What is better than love?

Love is placing our
happiness in the
happiness of another.

Lovers can be apart
over great distance,
but never in their hearts.

Every smile
was inspired by
another smile.
Every smile inspires
another smile.
Smile.

Nothing can

travel as far,

or as quickly,

as heartache.

When you travel,
always take with
you the memory
of a kiss.

You will know it is true
love because it will
find you, and when it
does it can never be
hidden again.

I shall send you
some kisses—
I know how very
much you like them.

Love is knowing when not to
jump off a bridge with someone,
and when to be at the bottom
ready to catch them.

Love is always there,
but you have to be able to see it.

No words are necessary
between loving hearts.

The memory of love never fades.

Love is having no breath to say the words you mean, and sending out a message with the eyes instead.

It is man's lot
to live life with
the knowledge
he will perish.
Love is all
we have of
immortality.

Love is a
two-way street.

The human heart is capable of feeling things the eyes will never see and things the mind will never understand.

We discover more about ourselves when we kiss someone else than we could ever have imagined possible.

The silence between lovers speaks a thousand words.

People who
are unsuited
to each other
stand out
like a pair of
unmatched
socks.
They look
awkward; they
feel awkward;
and one is
likely to wear
out before
the other.

There are as many ways to love as
there are lovers to love.

The memory of love often
outlasts the memory of lovers.

Love doesn't always come
along at a convenient time.

Who would choose to walk in the rain when they were offered the shelter of love?

A man is not where he lives,
but where he loves.

**Nothing tastes more
bitter than love that
remains unspoken.**

You can never love too much.

**If you would be happy
in love, give your love
where it is deserved.**

One can care little for man,
but we need a friend.

      Chinese proverb

To those we love best,
we can say the least.

You are, when all is said and
done, the sum of all you love.

Love and hate
are much closer
emotions than love
and indifference.

Signs of being in love:

Memorizing your favorite poem.

Suddenly having boundless energy.

Your feet don't touch the ground.

Everything looks beautiful.

You say "I love you"
and mean it.

Love deeply and passionately. You might get hurt, but it's the only way to live life completely.

Talk slow but think quick.

When you lose love, don't also lose
the lesson that love has taught you.

Love without risks is no love at all.

Love won easily may
also be lost easily.

War can't kill love,
but love can kill war.

He who walks in love
will wander far.

There is no
way of feeling
indifferent
about the
ending of love.
To lose love is
to have lived a
thousand lives,
then have them
all end at once.

We become, through life,
all that we have loved.

Love is like the wild rose-briar,
Friendship like the holly-tree—
The holly is dark when the rose-briar blooms
But which will bloom most constantly?

Emily Brontë

What other love is as intense
as unconsummated love?

Love is a game
which has no
rules, and, if
played fairly,
no losers.

The road to a lover's house
is never long.

The only place where love has no value is on the tennis court.

It is better to have loved and lost than never to have loved at all.

The love you give is the love you will receive.

Who do you turn to when
the only person in the
world who could stop
you from crying is the
one who made you cry?

Being in love is the greatest education.

A teddy bear teaches a child that love means being there when you're needed.

Do not be afraid to love too much. You can never run out of love.

One must learn to
be a sponge if one
wants to be loved by
hearts that overflow.

Give love when it is least deserved,
because that's when it's needed most.

Take time to love, or someone
else will do it for you.

True love is hard to find, hard to lose,
and impossible to forget.

Love walks in when the rest
of the world walks out.

Love is always being able
to forgive and forget.

Great love and great achievements
involve great effort.

True love may only come along once in a lifetime, so keep your eyes open for it!

Do not settle for somebody you can live with; find somebody you can't live without.

Love is a form of temporary insanity.

You don't get to choose love; it arrives one day and you just fall into it.